Weighing up the Evidence

TIMELINE:

The People's Republic of China

Dryad Press, London

Graham Thomas

Contents

© Graham Thomas 1990
First published 1990

Typeset by Tek-Art Ltd, Kent
and printed in Great Britain by
The Bath Press,
Bath, Avon,
for the Publishers
Dryad Press,
4 Fitzhardinge Street,
London W1H 0AH

ISBN 0 85219 791 8

The author and publishers thank the following for their
kind permission to reproduce copyright illustrations:
Camera Press for pages 13, 15 (bottom), 21, 23, 25, 28,
36, 42, 45, 46, 48, 52: Mary Evans Picture Library for
page 4; Hutchinson Library for page 22; Magnum for
the front cover (right) and pages 6, 7, 9, 15 (top), 17, 31;
Topham for page 38 and ET Archive for the front cover
(left).

The author would like to thank the following for their
help and advice in preparing this book: Hugh Baker, Tim
Barrett, Richard Edmonds, David Pollard, John Sargent,
Stuart Schram, Richard Tames and Ruth Taylor.

Front cover: Left: "The flowers are opening and
blooming in the new China", Chinese poster 1949.
Right: Students demonstrate in Tiananmen Square,
April 1989.

Introduction

Before modern times China was an agricultural country which had developed in relative isolation from the rest of the world to become one of the most prosperous and technologically advanced countries on earth. The Chinese had invented printing, paper money, gunpowder, the magnetic compass, and a host of other achievements. Indeed, they believed that theirs was the most civilized state and society in the known world, which for them meant East Asia (the Far East) and South East Asia. Their name for China was Zhong-guo (Chung Kuo), which means "Central Country" or "Middle Kingdom".

However from the 1840s onwards China was forced to open its doors to trade with the modern industrial West, spearheaded by Britain. In the 150 years or so since then, China's standing in the world has changed drastically for the worse. From being one of the world's richest countries, it finds itself backward; and from being a mighty empire without rivals to being one nation-state among many in a world overshadowed by the superpowers of the United States and the Soviet Union, and by the growing

Map of present-day China.

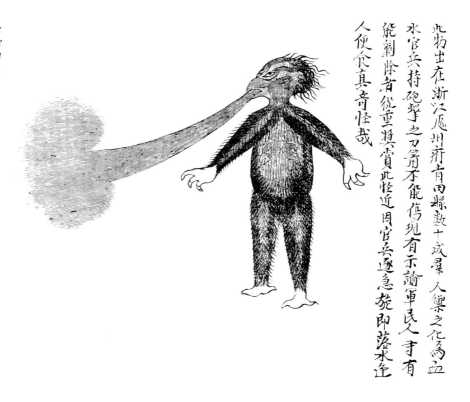

China's view of the West: A Qing dynasty cariacature of a fire-breathing English Sailor or "ocean devil".

此物出在浙江處州府有田縣數十成羣人藥之化為立
水官兵持砲擊之刀箭不能傷現有示諭軍民人才有
能剷除者從重與賞此怪近聞官兵逐急旋即落水逢
人便食真奇怪哉

industrial might of its neighbour Japan.

This book is organized around the theme of China's quest to regain the wealth and power which it has lost, focusing on the period since 1949. In working through the book from the standpoint of a historian, you need to bear in mind that the ways in which the Chinese see and experience the world are in important ways different from ours; that their ideas of what is right, good and possible both for the individual person and for society as a whole are also not the same as ours; and that their government and peasant-based economy have developed in their own very distinctive ways. You must be aware too that these ideas, values and institutions of the Chinese have evolved over more than two thousand years and that they are consequently very deep-rooted indeed. The interaction between them and the very different ideas, values and institutions thrust upon China by the modern industrial West is the stuff of modern Chinese history.

A note on the Chinese language

Chinese is written in characters, or ideograms, which give little or no indication of their pronunciation. In English, two systems of "romanization" are used to represent its sounds. The first is Pinyin, which is the standard Chinese romanization now used throughout the world and the more accurate guide to pronunciation. The second is the traditional Wade-Giles romanization which has been the standard in English-speaking countries for more than a century. When they first appear in this book, important

Punch, *22 December 1860. What do these two illustrations tell you about the attitudes of the Chinese and British towards one another during this period?*

WHAT WE OUGHT TO DO IN CHINA.

Chinese names and terms, with a few traditional exceptions, are printed in their Pinyin forms with the Wade-Giles equivalent in brackets, e.g. Guomindang (Kuomintang). Thereafter the Pinyin form only is used. Where a documentary extract uses the Wade-Giles form, the Pinyin equivalent is given in brackets, e.g. Hsin-min Pao (Xinmin Bao). Following standard Chinese practice, a person's family name is printed first, followed by his given name e.g. Mao (family name) Zedong (given name).

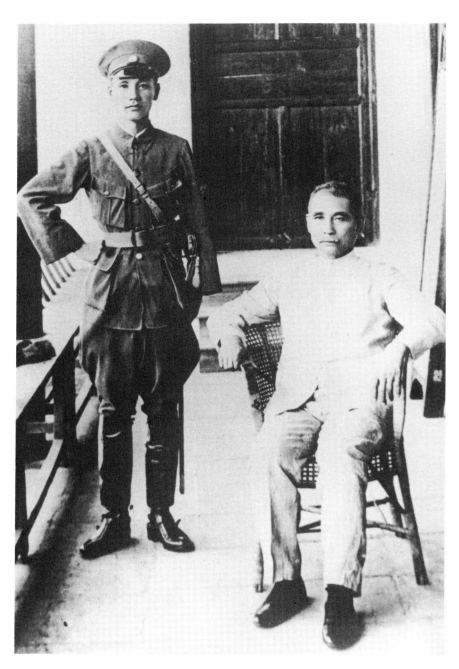

*Dr Sun Yat-sen (seated)
and Chiang Kai-shek
leaders of China's
Guomindang or
Nationalist Party, which
lost power in 1949.*

The Early Years of Communist Rule: 1949–55

THE ROAD TO RECOVERY

In 1949 the goal of a rich and strong China was in some ways more difficult to achieve than it had been in the nineteenth century. There were many more mouths to feed (540 million as against around 375 million in 1875), although the amount of land that could be used to grow food for them remained roughly the same, at about 15 per cent of the total land area. There was also the destruction caused by the long years of war against the Japanese as well as by the Chinese civil war: agricultural output in 1949, for example, was only two thirds of the previous highest recorded level. The Chinese Communist Party (CCP), under the leadership of Chairman Mao Zedong (Mao Tse-tung), faced a formidable task in trying to put China back on the road to wealth and strength.

The first months of "liberation" in Beijing

Derk Bodde, an American professor, was living in Beijing when the Communists took over in January 1949. These are extracts from his diary.

Currency (February 3, 1949)
Prices have dropped slightly, but it is obvious that few serious steps in this direction can be taken before the process of converting gold yuan [GY] into the new regime's "people's notes" [PY] has been completed . . . the exchange is set at GY\$10:PN\$1 for all persons save labourers, students, teachers, and "poor people". These . . . will be permitted to exchange up to GY\$500 apiece at the favoured rate of GY\$3:PY1.

Mao declares the founding of the People's Republic of China on 1 October 1949.

Industry

On the production front the papers are filled these days, quite *à la Russe*, with enthusiastic accounts of how the workers are rehabilitating industry to a point equal to, or even higher than, its pre-siege level.

Propaganda

Slogans and posters carrying [the authorities'] message now adorn all public places. Many, printed in bright colours are very effective, for example the one depicting a galloping cavalryman holding aloft a red banner, beneath which appears the caption: "Plant the victorious banner throughout China!"

(*Source:* quoted in *China Readings 3: Communist China*, ed. Franz Schurmann and Orville Schell, Pelican Books, 1968)

What problems were the Chinese Communists trying to solve by changing China's currency?

What is the significance of the phrase "à la Russe"?

The land and the peasants

Basic Programme on Chinese Agrarian Law Promulgated by the Central Committee of the Chinese Communist Party, 1947

China's agrarian system is unjust in the extreme. Speaking of general conditions, landlords and rich peasants who make up less than 10 per cent of the rural population hold approximately 70 to 80 per cent of the land, cruelly exploiting the peasantry. Farm labourers, poor peasants, middle peasants, and other people, however, who make up over 90 per cent of the land, hold a total of approximately only 20 to 30 per cent of the land, toiling throughout the whole year, knowing neither warmth nor full stomach. These grave conditions are the root of our country's being the victim of aggression, oppression, poverty, backwardness, and the basic obstacles to our country's democratization, industrialization independence, unity, strength and prosperity.

(*Source:* William Hinton, *Fanshen*, Pelican Books, 1972)

Whenever the Chinese Communists won control of a district in the civil war against the Guomindang (Kuomintang or Nationalist Party), they made systematic and thorough efforts to change "these grave conditions". As a start CCP cadres (officials) encouraged poor peasants to attend "speak bitterness" meetings and accuse landlords to their faces of all that they had suffered at their hands. In one North China village called Zhangshuang (Long Bow) a peasant called Shi Fu-yuan had this to say to his landlord Guo Chongwang at such a meeting:

In the famine year my brother worked for your family. We were all hungry. We had nothing to eat. But you had no thought for us. Several

Children queue for food during the winter of 1948-9. What does this picture suggest about the situation in China at this time?

times we tried to borrow grain from you. But it was all in vain. You watched us starve without pity.

(*Source:* William Hinton, op. cit.)

In June 1950 the CCP passed the Agrarian Reform Law. As a result, in village after village throughout China, landlords' and rich peasants' land was confiscated and shared out among the middle and poor peasants. These changes brought about a real social and political revolution in China's villages. The landlords were destroyed as a class and in the process many lost not only their land but their lives as well: one estimate suggests that 500,000 of them were killed. On the other hand the land reform did not mean equal shares of land for all. After it the average rich peasant owned and operated more than twice as much land as the average poor peasant. The main significance of the land reform was that it paved the way for the next wave of change that Mao and the CCP wanted to introduce on the land. This was aimed at creating a collectivized and ultimately industrialized agriculture.

CHINA'S EDUCATED PEOPLE: THE "INTELLECTUALS"

Next to the peasants, China's educated people, or intellectuals, were probably of the greatest concern to Mac Zedong and the CCP. Their knowledge and skills in government, industry and the education system were vital to China's progress. There were about four million of them during the mid-1950s in a population of about 600 million – a very much smaller proportion than in any Western country. Most came from well-off families and had been educated either in Western-style schools and universities in China or in the West itself, above all in America.

After 1949 Mao and the CCP organized special political campaigns like the Ideological Remoulding Movement of 1951-2 designed to ensure that intellectuals had the correct attitudes for the new China. In 1951 he said:

Ideological remoulding, primarily that of all types of intellectuals, is an important condition for the completion of democratic reforms in all fields and the gradual industrialization of our country.

(*Source: Selected Works of Mao Tsetung*, Vol. V, Foreign Languages Press, Peking, 1977)

The following extracts are from a confession made in 1952 by Professor Jin Yuelin, who had been a student at Harvard University in the United States and one of China's leading academic specialists in philosophy:

. . . I now consider the fundamental ideological source for my personal crust of selfishness to be the extremely depraved, epicurean, liberalist and bourgeois ideology of striving after individual freedom . . . . This kind of ideology was the ideology of the exploitative class . . . .

. . . I am a criminal for having sinned against the people. From now on, however, I shall strive to become a new man and a teacher of the people in substance as well as in name.

(*Source:* Robert Jay Lifton, *Thought Reform and the Psychology of Totalism*, Pelican, 1967)

What kind of attitudes was the CCP trying to encourage in China's educated people and why?

Do you think that someone like Professor Jin would have been more enthusiastic about helping to create a new China after going through such an "Ideological Remoulding Campaign" than before?

The first Five-Year Plan 1953-7

By 1953, with China well on the road to recovery, Mao Zedong and other CCP leaders could begin to put into practice their long-term strategy for making China rich and strong. Mao outlined his vision of the future in 1954:

> Our general objective is to strive to build a great socialist country . . . . It will probably take a period of three five-year plans, or fifteen years, to lay the foundation. Will China then become a great country? Not necessarily. I think for us to build a great socialist country, about fifty years, or ten five-year plans will probably be enough . . . . What can we make at present? We can make tables and chairs, teacups and teapots, we can grow grain and grind it into flour, and we can make paper. But we can't make a single motor car, plane, tank or tractor. So we mustn't brag and be cocky.
>
> (*Source: Selected Works of Mao Tsetung*, Vol. V, Foreign Languages Press, Peking, 1977)

Mao and his comrades in the CCP had in fact decided to adopt the Soviet Union's model of economic development. How useful do you think Soviet experience was likely to be for China?

Agriculture and the Plan

In June 1949 Mao Zedong had set out the Party's strategy for agriculture:

> The peasant economy is scattered and the socialization of agriculture, judging by the Soviet Union's experience, will require a long time and painstaking work. Without socialization of agriculture, there can be no complete, consolidated socialism. The steps to socialize agriculture must be coordinated with the development of a powerful industry having state enterprise as its backbone.
>
> (*Source: Selected Works of Mao Tsetung*, Vol. IV, Foreign Languages Press, Peking, 1969)

What did Mao mean by the "socialization of agriculture"? Why did he believe that it was necessary and would take a long time?

Already in the early 1950s the CCP had begun to organize the peasants first into "mutual aid teams", to which they contributed their labour, working animals like buffaloes, and tools. Then in 1954-5, under the Plan, they began to be formed into larger units called "Semisocialist" or "Lower Stage Agricultural Producers' Co-operatives" (APCs), to which the members contributed their land as well, although in theory keeping their individual ownership. About one third of the peasants were expected to be in the APCs by the end of the plan in 1957.

The next stage was to be the fully socialist Higher Stage Co-operatives rather like the collective farms in the Soviet Union, in which the land was owned by the co-operative, not by the individual peasants. According to the Plan it would take 15 years to reach this stage.

Industry and the Plan

On 1 January 1953, the first official day of the Plan, the *People's Daily* declared:

Industrialization provides a guarantee that our people shall no longer be exposed by imperialism to treachery and humiliations, and shall no longer live in poverty.

Why did the CCP believe that industrialization would provide such a guarantee?

In its targets for industry the Plan was extremely ambitious: there was to be a headlong dash to build around 700 heavy state industrial plants, 156 with aid from the Soviet Union, which had to be paid for. Some CCP leaders wanted China to specialize in agriculture and light industry (the industrial revolution and modern economic growth in Britain and Japan, for example, had been based on the development of light industries such as textile manufacturing). But Mao was determined to take the Soviet path and those of this colleagues who wanted a strong heavy industrial base on which to build a defence industry in China supported him.

The money required to develop heavy industry was to come from the profits of industry itself, as well as from the taxes which the government raised from agriculture and private industry. Living standards for most people would have to remain low as there would be few resources left over to manufacture consumer goods.

In early July the First Five Year Plan was made public. All could now see that China had a clear strategy for economic development which aimed to raise her steadily, step by step, to the level of advanced industrial nations in about fifty years.

ON REFLECTION:

How different might the CCP's strategy have been if the United States had contributed to China's economic development, as Mao had hoped they would in 1945?

What can you find out about how, for example, Japan and India set about the task of economic development after the Second World War? How did their situations differ from that of China?

Mao and the Road to Wealth and Strength: 1956-9

MAO SPEEDS UP THE COLLECTIVIZATION OF AGRICULTURE

On 31 July 1955 Mao Zedong made a speech entitled "on the co-operative transformation of agriculture" to a conference of Communist Party officials from all over China:

China has an enormous population with insufficient cultivated land . . . natural calamities are frequent . . . and farming methods are backward. Consequently, although the life of the peasant masses has improved since the agrarian reform . . . many are still in difficulty or not well off and those who are well off are relatively few . . . .

(*Source: Selected Works of Mao Tsetung*, Volume V, Foreign Languages Press, Peking, 1977)

Mao's strategy for improving the backwardness of China's agriculture was to consolidate the existing small co-operatives into much larger, he hoped much more productive, units. Despite the doubts of some of its leaders the CCP put the new policy into action. The effect was dramatic: by March 1956 over 90 per cent of the peasants were in co-operatives, and by 1957 almost all were in the 680,000 Higher Stage Co-operatives. A transformation that was planned to take 15 years was carried out in little more than 12 months.

A production team meeting. How difficult would it have been to persuade people to work together in teams like this?

After the rapid collectivization of 1956 Mao expected dramatic increases in production. But he was mistaken. By the autumn of 1957 it was clear that agriculture was still not growing fast enough, while unemployment in the towns remained a serious problem.

In Mao's view the Soviet Union had been a valuable model for China to copy so far. But now, he declared, China could do better than the Russians.

Mao launches the "Great Leap Forward"

Mao's solution to doing better than the Russians and other foreign countries was even more drastic and dramatic than the accelerated collectivization of 1956. He decided to launch a huge campaign that would take China to a new peak of economic achievement in a very short time. He was quite clear where the motive force was going to come from for this new movement. At the Eighth CCP Congress in Beijing during May 1958 Mao said:

Our method is to lift the lid, break down superstition, and let the initiative and creativity of the labouring people explode.

(*Source: Miscellany of Mao Tsetung Thought (1949-1968)*, Joint Publication Research Service: Translations on Communist China, quoted in Roderick MacFarquhar, *The Origins of the Cultural Revolution*, OUP, 1983)

Why did Mao Zedong think that "the labouring people" were so important for China's economic progress?

How and why does Mao's attitude to "the labouring people" differ from his attitude to educated people or "intellectuals"?

Mao rallies support for the Great Leap

Mao toured China to encourage local Party cadres to participate whole-heartedly in the new movement. His own enthusiasm and optimism knew no bounds:

Throughout the country, the communist spirit is surging forward . . . . Apart from their other characteristics, China's 600 million people have two remarkable peculiarities; they are, first of all, poor, and secondly, blank. That may seem like a bad thing, but it is really a good thing. Poor people want change, want to do things, want revolution. A clean sheet of paper has no blotches, and so the newest and most beautiful words can be written on it, the newest and most beautiful pictures can be painted on it.

(*Source:* Ed. Stuart R. Schram, *The Political Thought of Mao Tse-tung*, New York, 1969, quoted in Wilson, *People's Emperor*)

The Great Leap in agriculture: the coming of Peoples' Communes

During April in Henan province 27 Agricultural Producers' Co-operatives were merged into a single huge co-operative, or "People's Commune", of

Commune members make their own sewage system.

Commune members labour to build a canal during the Great Leap. What might be the advantages and disadvantages of using peasant labour in this way?

more than 9000 households. By November things had gone at lightning speed: about 26,000 communes had been formed, each containing between 2000 and 5000 households or 10-25,000 people.

In October the *People's Daily* reported that many communes had introduced a system of free meals, while others had gone even further:

Some people's communes operate a system of "seven guarantees" or "ten guarantees", under which members are guaranteed meals, clothes, housing, schooling, medical attention, burial, haircuts, theatrical entertainment, money for heating in winter and money for weddings.... It ... represents a step towards "selflessness". Therefore it belongs to the sphere of communism and is a germination of communism.

(*Source: People's Daily*, 1 October, quoted in MacFarquhar, *Origins of the Cultural Revolution*, Vol. 2)

Why do you think some communes introduced the system of "guarantees"?

The Great Leap in industry: steel fever

At the Eighth Party Congress in May 1958 Mao said:

Neither do I understand industry. I know nothing about it, yet I do not believe that it is unattainable. I discussed the subject with several persons in charge of industry. It seems to be incomprehensible at the beginning, but becomes comprehensible after a few years of study. There's nothing much to it!

(*Source: Miscellany of Mao Tse-tung Thought*, Part 1, quoted in Wilson, *People's Emperor*)

In 1957 China's steel production had been 5.35 million tons with a target of 6.2 million tons for 1958. In June Mao decided that 10.7 million tons was possible. An all-out drive to reach this new national target then swept over China.

In the far south of China an English visitor saw the steel campaign in action in the province of Yunnan:

We walked through the paddy to another village where four monstrous home-made blast furnaces had been rigged up. The place was a furious, seething, clattering scene of frenzy. People carried baskets of ore, people stoked, people goaded buffalo carts, people tipped cauldrons of white hot metal, people stood on rickety ladders and peered into furnaces, people wheeled barrows of crude metal – though to me the stuff that was being poured out at the bottom of the furnaces looked exactly like the stuff that was being poured in at the top.

(*Source:* MacFarquhar, op. cit., Vol. 2)

The Great Leap and education

In China educated people – those who had been to school and university and therefore worked with their brains – had always looked down on peasants and workers, who worked with their hands. Mao believed that one of the keys to the success of the Great Leap was to change their

Workers, many of them from Beijing, building a dam during the Great Leap. Why are there so many people and so few machines in this picture?

contemptuous attitude to manual work. He therefore recommended that school and university students wherever possible should do manual work as part of their education. In September Mao said in a speech:

> If schools run factories, factories run schools, schools run farms, and communes run schools . . . then study and manual labour will be integrated.

(*Source:* MacFarquhar, *Origins*, Vol. 2)

Students everywhere threw themselves into the campaign to make steel. They collected scrap and pig iron for the furnaces. By August it was said that 18 colleges in 11 cities were able to refine 700,000 tons of steel, while in the cities of Nanjing and Guangzhou 34 secondary schools each had some kind of furnace. Liu Shaoqi, one of the most important leaders of the CCP after Mao, was taken aback the following year when his own nine year-old son returned home exhausted after working for eight hours.

Why did Mao believe that study and manual work should be "integrated"?

On 1 October 1958, China's National Day, the *People's Daily* proclaimed:

> In agriculture the Red Flag is flying . . . emerging into the red flames coming from the steel plants: the sky has turned red . . . . Today, in the era of Mao Tse-tung, heaven is here on earth . . . . Once the Party calls, tens of millions of the masses jump into motion. Chairman Mao is a great prophet.
>
> (*Source:* quoted in Wilson, *People's Emperor*)

The first results of the Great Leap are announced

The results of this extraordinary movement appeared to be astonishing. At the end of the year it was announced that the 1958 grain harvest was 375 million tons, more than double that for 1957. It was also announced that the 10.7 million ton steel target had been achieved in mid-December. Production increases were later reported for coal (108 per cent), crude oil (55 per cent) and electricity (42 per cent).

The "initiative and creativity of the labouring people", which Mao Zedong believed in so fervently, indeed seemed to have "exploded" to China's enormous benefit. At the end of 1958 a rich and powerful China seemed much nearer than it had a year before.

Compare the way in which the Chinese were trying to develop China economically in the years 1953-56 (see previous chapter) with the approach during the Great Leap Forward. What were the main differences? How do you explain them?

MAO AND THE INTELLECTUALS

By 1956 many of China's educated people were no longer so enthusiastic about life in a Communist China. They resented not having the freedom to express their opinions openly, especially their criticisms of the Communist Party. Mao therefore started to ease the pressure on the intellectuals and to encourage them to speak more freely. In a speech of February 1957 he said:

> People may ask, since Marxism is accepted as the guiding ideology by the majority of the people in our country, can it be criticized? Certainly it can. Marxism is scientific truth and fears no criticism. . . . Plants raised in

hothouses are unlikely to be hardy. Carrying out the policy of letting a hundred flowers blossom and a hundred schools of thought contend will not weaken, but strengthen the leading position of Marxism in the ideological field.

What should our policy be towards non-Marxist ideas? . . . Will it do to ban such ideas and deny them any opportunity for expression? Certainly not.

(*Source: Selected Works of Mao Tse-tung*, Vol. V)

What do you think Mao meant by "the policy of letting a hundred flowers blossom and a hundred schools of thought contend"?

Why did he believe that this policy would "strengthen the leading position of Marxism"?

China's intellectuals speak out

It took three months or so before intellectuals began to believe that they could say what they thought openly. When they did their criticisms came in a flood. A group of economists, for example, produced a manifesto in which they said:

Our financial and economic policies and measures have either been borrowed blindly from Soviet Russia's precedents or have been sheer trial and error, subjectivism and recklessness personified, based on no objective economic laws whatsoever and in any case we do not know what laws there are worth following . . . .

(*Source:* Roderick MacFarquhar, *The Hundred Flowers Campaign and the Chinese Intellectuals*, Octagon Books, New York, 1974)

Students were especially active. In Beijing University they started a "Democratic Wall" and put up posters presenting their views in all their variety. The government news agency reported that some of them had founded a "Hundred Flowers Society" and that:

The key members of the society have openly declared that their purpose was not to help the Party in its rectification campaign, but to initiate a "movement for freedom and democracy", a "movement for the thorough reform of the political system". They cry, "Marxism is out of date" . . . . They suggest "learning from the democracy and freedom of the capitalist countries" . . . .

(*Source:* MacFarquhar, *Hundred Flowers*)

At universities in other cities of China, such as Wuhan, students were saying similar things and organizing protest demonstrations and strikes.

Why were intellectuals and students so critical of the Chinese Communist Party?

Mao clamps down on intellectuals

In June Mao Zedong's speech of February (page 18) was printed and published. When intellectuals all over China came to read it they found the following passage, which does not seem to have been in the original:

... what should be the criteria today for distinguishing fragrant flowers from poisonous weeds? ... Words and deeds ... should ... be beneficial, and not harmful, to socialist transformation and socialist construction ... help to strengthen, and not shake off or weaken, the leadership of the Communist Party ....

(*Source: Selected Works of Mao Tse-tung*, Vol. V)

What were the main differences in Mao Zedong's mind between "fragrant flowers" and "poisonous weeds"?

In the summer of 1957 the Chinese Communist leaders initiated an "Anti-Rightist Campaign" to frighten critics of the regime into silence. In August three leaders of the student movement in the important city of Wuhan in central China were sentenced to death and executed. Hundreds of other executions were reported from all over China during this period.

Several hundred thousand people who were regarded as opponents and potential opponents by the Communists were sent to camps for "education through labour", even though they had committed no crime. They were deprived of their civil and political rights and forced to do hard physical work. At the same time they had to confess to the sin of criticizing the Communist Party and learn the correct, positive attitudes required by a citizen of Communist China. Most of these people, even when released from camps, did not regain full civil and political rights until the 1980s.

ON REFLECTION:

Why do you think Mao Zedong changed to a "crash campaign" approach to economic development for China from the mid-1950s?

The Great Leap Forward:
The Facts Emerge 1959-60

**THE SITUATION
ON THE
COMMUNES**

These are extracts from letters written by peasants living on communes in the south-eastern provinces of Guangdong and Fujian to their relatives in South East Asian countries such as Malaysia and Indonesia. Some date from as early as October 1958:

A terraced hillside in Shanxi Province. Why is it necessary to farm the land so intensively?

Property
With the establishment of communes, all property has become State-owned; all houses and furniture have been turned into Government property. They merely do what they like. No one has any rights at all . . . .

Food
For months we have not tasted a catty [1.1lbs/500g.] of meat or a single piece of fish. Everybody is in the same situation. Nothing edible is procurable . . . .

(*Source:* quoted in MacFarquhar, *Origins*, Vol. 2)

There was a very good harvest in 1958. Why then was there such a shortage of food?

THE LEADERS   In late December Mao Zedong and other Party leaders in Beijing and in the provinces began to realize that people in the cities were going short of food because not enough was being brought in from the countryside. Later it became clear that members of the richer brigades in some Communes resented having to share grain and property with poorer brigades so that everyone gct more or less equal shares of everything. They therefore kept as much of their harvest as they dared for their own use and began to work less hard.

In other Communes there were not enough hands to harvest the crops as Marshal Peng Dehuai (Peng Teh-huai) found when he visited Gansu (Kansu) province. In one village he noticed a large pile of ripe crops left lying on the ground. When asked why this was, an old peasant explained to him that all the able-bodied people were busy trying to set records for steel production. Peng said to him:

A 'backyard' steel furnace in action.   Hasn't any one of you given a thought to what you will eat next year if you

Mao tours a commune in Hopei province during the Great Leap Forward.

don't bring in the crops? You're never going to eat steel!

The old peasant's reply was

True enough; who would disagree with that? But . . . who can stand up against this wind?

PROBLEMS WITH STEEL

In December 1958 it was officially admitted that of the 10.7 million tons produced that year only 9 million were of useable quality, a figure which was later reduced to 8 million. Mao was forced to admit:

I made a mistake at the Peitaiho [Beidaihe] Conference. Concentrating on the 10.7 million tons of steel, the people's commune . . . I did not think of other things. The Peitaiho Conference resolution must now be revised. I was enthusiastic at the time, and failed to combine revolutionary fervour and the practical spirit . . . .

(*Source:* MacFarquhar, *Origins*, Vol. 2)

AGRICULTURE: REALITY BREAKS IN

In April Mao Zedong also wrote a letter to be circulated throughout the Communist Party in which he wrote:

Fixing production targets must be based on realities. Just do not pay any attention to those stipulations made in the instructions from higher levels.

Ignore them and simply concentrate on practical possibilities . . . . State exatly how much you have harvested and refrain from making false statements which are contrary to facts. There must be honesty . . . .

(*Source:* MacFarquhar, *Origins*, Vol. 2)

How do you think a lower level Communist Party official working in the countryside would have felt after reading this letter?

MARSHAL PENG DEHUAI CRITICIZES THE GREAT LEAP FORWARD

In July 1959 Chairman Mao Zedong and other top CCP leaders held a conference at Lushan in Jiangxi (Kiangsi) province. All of them knew by now that the increase in agricultural production claimed for 1958 had been grossly exaggerated. There were also signs that 1959 would not bring a good harvest. The north-east had already had six months of drought, while spring had brought floods to several provinces: in Guangdong (Kwangtung) they were the worst for a hundred years. And another drought was just beginning which would devastate the autumn harvest.

Peng Dehuai had seen for himself the results of the Great Leap Forward. He felt that he had to speak out against it. That would mean in effect criticizing Chairman Mao Zedong, the launcher of the Leap and the most powerful man in China.

Peng's chosen way of speaking out was to write and distribute a long "letter of opinion" to the Lushan conference. On the subject of the backyard steel campaign he wrote:

In the nationwide campaign for the production of iron and steel, too many small blast furnaces were built with a waste of material, money and manpower . . . .

(*Source: Memoirs of a Chinese Marshal*, trans. Zhong Longpu, Foreign Languages Press, Beijing, 1984)

Peng then discussed the reasons why he thought the Great Leap Forward had gone wrong:

The job of autumn harvesting was handled crudely and without consideration of cost, and we considered ourselves rich while actually we were still poor.

(*Source: The Case of Peng Teh-huai 1959-1968*, Union Research Institute, Hong Kong, 1968)

. . . we were thinking of entering a communist society in one stride, and the idea of trying to be the first to do this gained an upper hand in our minds for a time . . . .

(*Source: Memoirs of a Chinese Marshal*)

How much of Peng's letter is a criticism of Mao Zedong himself?

MAO FIGHTS BACK

Mao's retaliation was swift. Peng was accused of being a member of an anti-Party clique and replaced as Defence Minister by Marshal Lin Biao (Lin Piao). Several of the top military men of the PLA (People's Liberation Army)

Mao and his new second-in-command, Marshal Lin Biao.

who were associated with him were either transferred or removed. A month later he wrote another letter, this time to Mao, in which he said:

> .... Now, I have profoundly realized that my bourgeois outlook and methodology are deep-rooted and my individualism is exceedingly serious. Now I have also realized how great a price the Party and the people have paid to foster a person like me and how horrible would be the danger if I were not exposed and criticized so thoroughly in time ... I have failed the Party, failed the people and also failed you ....

(*Source: The Case of Peng Teh-Huai*)

Why did Peng feel it necessary to write this confession? Compare it with Professor Jin's (see page 10).

MAO ON THE DEFENSIVE

Although only Peng Dehuai had directly and openly criticized the Great Leap, Mao knew that many other leading members of the CCP had serious doubts about it. He tried to win them over in a speech he made at Lushan. He said defiantly:

> Just because for a time there were too few vegetables, too few hair-pins, no soap, a lack of balance in the economy and tension in the market, everyone became tense ... I did not see any reason for tension ....

I am a complete outsider when it comes to economic construction, I understand nothing about industrial planning . . . . Comrades, in 1958 and 1959 the main responsibility was mine, and you should take me to task . . . .

(*Source: Miscellany of Mao Tse-tung Thought* Part 1, quoted in Dick Wilson, *The People's Emperor*)

THE STATISTICAL RETREAT

The final report of the Lushan conference contained the revised figures for the results of the Great Leap Forward in 1958. Grain output was recorded as 250 million tons (not the 375 million tons claimed at the time); cotton as 2.1 million tons (not 3.35 million); steel as 8 million tons (not 11.08 million), with 3.08 million tons from backyard furnaces considered as of poor quality. The report also published the revised production targets for 1959: 275 (not 525) million tons of grain; 2.31 (not 5) million tons of cotton, and 8 (not 12) million tons of steel. Mao's conclusion was as follows:

The moral is that one must not capitulate in the face of difficulties. Things like people's communes and collective mess halls have deep economic roots. They should not, nor can they, be blown away by a gust of wind . . . .

(*Source:* MacFarquahar, *Origins*, Vol. 2)

On 29 August the *People's Daily* newspaper published a long article entitled "Long live the People's Communes" and a few days later another which declared:

Now every province in the whole country is dotted everywhere with iron and steel plants of different sizes . . . . Molten iron flows like water; the sparks of steel splash all around.

(*Source:* MacFarquhar, *Origins*, Vol. 2)

What do you think the public, official view of the Great Leap Forward was at this stage?

SOVIET SCIENTISTS AND ENGINEERS ARE CALLED HOME FROM CHINA

But other, political, sparks were beginning to fly from the autumn of 1959, because China's relations with its main ally the Soviet Union under its leader Nikita Khrushchev had begun to go sour.

The dispute took some time to come to a head, but by the spring a bitter slanging match had developed. The Chinese accused the Soviets of abandoning Marxism-Leninism. Khrushchev denounced the Chinese Communists as madmen who wanted to unleash war and accused Mao Zedong of being "an ultra-Leftist, spinning theories detached from the realities of the modern world".

In July the bombshell came: the Soviet Union ordered all of its scientists and technical experts to leave China within one month. This decision took both China's leaders and the 1390 Soviet experts then working in the country completely by surprise. It was a bitter blow to the Chinese because the Soviets in many cases left half-finished factories and mines in China, taking the plans with them.

Their going was a serious setback for China's economic development. Over the previous 10 years the Soviet Union had sent almost 11,000 experts to China together with all the machinery, equipment and blueprints for building more than 300 industrial plants of all kinds including an atomic reactor. In addition more than 13,000 Chinese had been sent to the Soviet Union for scientific education and technical training. By 1957 China's heavy industry had been rebuilt with Soviet help and much of its administration, armed forces, educational system and science had been remodelled along Soviet lines.

The Chinese had now lost their main source of advanced scientific knowledge and technological knowhow which they needed to make China a modern country. Some Chinese leaders were very worried by the Soviet withdrawal. One or two were even said to have discussed turning to the West for technology instead. But this possibility was never explored. The Chinese were now on their own.

ON REFLECTION:

What conclusions can be drawn from the Great Leap Forward about:

i) Chinese society and Chinese attitudes?

ii) Mao Zedong's character?

iii) Chinese politics?

China under Liu Shaoqi and Deng Xiaoping: 1960-65

MAO TAKES A BACK SEAT

Liu Shaoqi becomes Head of State

In the months after the Lushan conference Mao Zedong retired from active leadership. Liu Shaoqi (Liu Shao-ch'i) became Head of State in his place and among his colleagues in the front line was Deng Xiaoping (Teng Hsiao-ping), the General Secretary of the CCP who was to become the most powerful man in China during the 1980s. With Government Premier Zhou Enlai (Chou Ēn-lai) they were now in day-to-day charge of China's affairs.

1960-62

The three bitter years

China's new head of state Liu Shaoqi, seen here receiving delegates from the National Students Congress in 1960

As late as January 1959 the officially-announced target for grain production was 525 million tons, but in the event the peasants brought in less than 180 million. In 1960 things took a turn for the worse. There was widespread drought in some provinces and exceptionally severe typhoons and floods in others. China was now facing its worst agricultural disaster for a century.

Peasant soldiers visiting their home villages on leave from the PLA found their families hungry and were angry:

At present what the peasants eat in the villages is even worse than what dogs ate in the past. At that time dogs ate chaff and grain. Now the people are too hungry to work and pigs are too hungry to stand up. Commune members ask: "Is Chairman Mao going to allow us to starve to death?"

(*Source:* Cheng, *The Politics of the Chinese Red Army*, quoted in MacFarquhar, *Origins*, Vol. 2)

But no one, not even Chairman Mao, could conjure food out of thin air. In one county of Guangdong province in south-east China 20,000 people starved to death. In 1960 China's population actually fell by 4.5% and the famine of 1961-2 was later said to be the worst since 1879. It has been estimated that up to 43,000,000 people died following the Great Leap Forward.

How far were China's problems at this time a result of the Great Leap Forward?

1961-1965   A period of recovery

The aim of Liu Shaoqi, Deng Xiaoping, Zhou Enlai, Chen Yun and others was to restore the balance between the different sectors of China's economy which the Great Leap Forward had so disrupted. The relationship they felt was most necessary to get right was that between agriculture and industry. They were certain that the surplus produced by agriculture was the key to economic progress. Without it there would be no resources to develop industry or the economy generally.

They therefore chose a strategy of "taking agriculture as the foundation, industry as the leading factor". This meant in practice treating agriculture as the most important sector of the economy followed by light industry and heavy industry.

Since agriculture was the first priority for Liu Shaoqi and his colleagues they made many important changes in the countryside. Land was still collectively, not privately, owned and most of it was used to grow crops which had to be sold to the government at fixed prices. But the team was the basic work group as well as the level at which the accounting was done. But in some areas teams made agreements to hand over tasks such as raising livestock, forestry or maintaining farm tools to small groups, such as households, or individuals: this was known as the "responsibility system" and the land used was called "small freedoms land".

It also became much easier again for peasants to use a certain percentage of their team's land (about 5-7 per cent) to grow crops or raise animals which they could sell privately in small free markets for higher prices than the government would pay. By 1962 30 per cent of the grain production was coming from these private plots and a large proportion of China's vegetables, fruit, poultry, eggs and pork.

An internal Party report of 1962 from Lianjiang County in Fujian province had this to say about the improved conditions in the area:

Two different points of view exist concerning the reason for these improved conditions. The majority of the people believe that the improvement is due to party leadership, the strength of policies, and state support. Some, however, are confused in their ideology and say that these favourable conditions have resulted from the "small freedoms"; others say that these conditions result from the use of private plots . . . and free markets . . . .

. . . . Although we have collectivized, domestic industries and private plots still exist . . . . They are supplements to the collective economy, required by the collectives, which we cannot do away with. However, they are also capable, at each instant, of giving rise to capitalism and bringing about the struggle between the two roads . . . .

(*Source:* Wang Hung-chih, "Implementation of the Resolutions of the Tenth Plenum of the Eighth Central Committee on Strengthening the Collective Economy and Expanding Agricultural Production" quoted in ed. Mark Selden, *The People's Republic of China*, Monthly Review Press, New York and London, 1979)

Why does the report say that they cannot do away with domestic industries and private plots?

What do the authors of the report dislike about private plots?

Changes in agriculture 1957-1965

	Chemical fertiliser	Irrigation and drainage equipment	Tractors
	(million tons)	------(million horsepower)------	
1957	0.8	0.6	0.4
1962	2.8	6.1	1.5
1963	3.9	6.9	1.7
1964	5.8	7.6	1.8
1965	7.6	9.1	2.2

(*Source:* Thomas G Rawski, *China Quarterly*, No.53, January–March 1973 quoted in Riskin, *China's Political Economy*, OUP, 1987)

What does this table tell you about the aims of Liu Shaoqi and his colleagues for agriculture and industry and the results achieved?

To achieve their aims for industry Liu and his colleagues took away the power which the Great Leap Forward had given to local authorities to run their factories and other economic enterprises in their own way. China was once again much more of a "command economy", centrally planned and controlled from Beijing. But it was in too poor a state for a third five year plan to be introduced as it should have been officially in 1963. Until 1966 planning could only be done one year at a time.

To help shift the balance from industry to agriculture Lin and his colleagues cut back or stopped many of the heavy industrial projects started during the Great Leap. To improve industry's performance a system

The electrical plant in Shenyang, where in order to keep to the required level of production during the Great Leap, only those of the 4500 workers who lived in distant provinces were allowed holidays.

of payment was brought back into the factories, based upon individual incentives. Workers were again paid piece rates and bonuses, so that the more they produced, the more they were paid. Even so, the difference between the highest and lowest wages remained fairly small.

Changes in China's foreign trade

Exports (US$ million)	*Socialist Countries*	*Capitalist Countries*	*Total*
1959	1595	615	2205
1962	920	605	1525
1964	730	1040	1770
Imports			
1959	1365	695	2060
1962	490	660	1150
1964	395	1080	1475

(*Source:* Robert L Price, *Communist China's Balance of Payments, 1950-65* in US Congress, Joint Economic Committee 1967, quoted in Riskin, *China's Political Economy*)

How and why did the pattern of China's foreign trade change 1959-1964?

THE DEBATE ABOUT WHAT TO DO NEXT

The emergency programme of "readjustment" and "consolidation" which Liu Shaoqi and Deng Xiaoping had introduced after 1961 took three or four years to put the economy back on its feet. It was then time for China's political leaders and economic specialists to work out a long-term strategy to put China once again on what they believed was the right road to wealth and strength. No one could be satisfied with things as they were.

There were three different approaches. Liu Shaoqi and Deng Xiaoping were in favour of keeping a tight grip on the economy from Beijing. By doing this they had already succeeded in repairing most of the damage done by the Great Leap. Some of China's professional economists favoured increasing the scope for individual enterprise and expanding free markets. This promised faster economic growth. Peasants, for example, seemed to work harder and more productively on their private plots because they knew they could sell the produce in a local free market and keep the profit for themselves. A third view was that of Mao Zedong.

MAO STARTS TO BECOME ACTIVE AGAIN

Mao was becoming increasingly restless as he saw the direction which China was taking under Liu Shaoqi and Deng Xiaoping. He felt that their policies were taking China away from the kind of socialism that he believed in, and could well result in the country becoming capitalist. Late in 1962 he therefore initiated a campaign called the Socialist Education Campaign with the aim of promoting socialist attitudes and reversing the tide set in motion by Liu and Deng. However they successfully undermined it.

Mao's feelings about the way things were going became even stronger as time went by. In May, 1963 the Central Committee of the Communist Party passed the following resolution drafted under his direction:

> Landlords and rich peasants who have been overthrown are employing all kinds of schemes in an attempt to corrupt our cadres in order to usurp the leadership and power. In some communes and brigades the leadership and power actually have fallen into their hands . . . .
>
> In commerce, the activities of speculation and profiteering have reached serious proportions . . . .
>
> The phenomena of exploiting hired hands, high-interest loans, buying and selling of land have also occurred . . . .
>
> These facts have combined to give us a most serious lesson: never at any moment should we forget class struggle, forget the proletarian dictatorship, forget to rely on the poor and the lower middle peasants, forget the party policies, forget party work.

(*Source:* ed. Selden op. cit.)

Why did Mao want everyone to understand thoroughly the problem of classes and class struggle?

Mao's concern about China's younger generation

In the summer of 1964 Mao had long conversations with his nephew Mao Yuanxin, a student at a military engineering institute in North China, and explained to him:

> The basic idea of Marxism-Leninism is that you must carry out revolution. But what is revolution? Revolution is the proletariat overthrowing the capitalists, the peasants over-throwing the landlords,

and then afterwards setting up a workers' and peasants' political power
. . . . At present, the task of the revolution has not yet been completed; it
has not yet been finally determined who, in the end, will overthrow
whom . . . .

(*Source:* ed. Schram, *Mao Tse-tung Unrehearsed*)

A few weeks later Mao said at a conference that teachers and students in higher education should extend their class education by spending time with the peasants in the countryside:

People won't die by going down to the countryside. There may be some
'flu but it will be all right when they put on more clothes . . . . Everybody
should go: professors, instructors, administrative workers and students
for a period of five months at a time. They should spend five months in
rural areas and five months in factories to acquire some perceptual
knowledge. They should take a look at horses, cows, sheep, chickens,
dogs and pigs, as well as rice, kaoliang, legumes, wheat and millet.

(*Source: Miscellany of Mao Tse-tung Thought*, Part II, quoted in Wilson, *People's Emperor*)

Why was Mao so concerned that teachers should spend the time in the countryside?

In early 1965 Mao tried again to make the Socialist Education Campaign into a movement to achieve what he believed were the correct attitudes and philosophy throughout the Communist Party. He was able, as before, to get the Central Committee of the Communist Party to issue a directive which came to be known as the "Twenty-Three Points". It argued that action should be taken to deal with "capitalist roaders" in the Party and government, who he described as the "bureaucratic class" who were:

sharply opposed to the working class and the poor and lower-middle
peasants. These people have become or are in the process of becoming
bourgeois elements sucking the blood of the workers. How can they have
proper understanding?

(*Source:* Wilson, *People's Emperor*)

What does Mao mean by the "bureaucratic class"?

Why does he say that it is "sharply opposed to the working class and the poor and lower-middle peasants"?

But when it came to putting his aims into action, Mao again found himself blocked by Liu Shaoqi, Deng Xiaoping and their supporters. His only support came from Lin Biao (Lin Piao), the Defence Minister and Commander-in-Chief of the PLA.

Mao's concluded that he would never get his way in Beijing as things were: he would have to change his strategy. Just as he had after the Great Leap Forward, therefore, he decided to go south to Shanghai, China's second and biggest city. But this time he went not to enjoy the climate but to join forces with his wife, Jiang Qing (Chiang Ching), and her political friends Zhang Chunqiao (Chang Ch'un-ch'iao), Yao Wenyuan, Wang Hongwen (Wang Hung-wen), and many others. They were all ardent supporters of Mao and helped him to make Shanghai his power-base. Mao did not return to Beijing for nine months. What he and his followers planned during that time only became clear during the summer of 1966.

ON REFLECTION:

Why did Liu and Deng consistently prevent Mao from doing what he wanted with the Socialist Education Campaign?

Why did Mao believe that "the task of the revolution is not yet complete" (see page 33)?

Why was he so concerned about China's young people?

The Great Proletarian Cultural Revolution and After 1966-78

From June 1966 a huge, new political campaign burst over China called the Great Proletarian Cultural Revolution. It had several aims:

> The struggle against the capitalist roaders in the Party is the principal task, but not the object. The object is to solve the problem of world outlook and eradicate revisionism . . . .
> . . . . The proletarian Revolution is a revolution to abolish all exploiting classes and all systems of exploitation; it is a most through-going revolution to bring about the gradual elimination of the differences between workers and peasants, between town and country, and between mental and manual labour. This cannot but meet with the most stubborn resistance from the exploiting classes.

(*Source:* From a talk by Mao with an Albanian military delegation, quoted in ed. Milton, Milton and Schurmann)

How did Mao and his supporters expect to achieve these aims?

MAO'S NEW WEAPON

The Red Guards

The Cultural Revolution proper lasted until early 1969. In its early stages Mao Zedong took an extraordinary step: he called upon the university and secondary school students of China to help him to attack the "four olds" – old ideas, old culture, old customs and old habits – and all those regarded as "revisionists" in their schools, universities and the Communist Party itself. Everyone in authority then became a target for the students. In July Mao said to members of the Central Committee:

> The young people are the main force of the cultural revolution. They must be fully mobilized.

(*Source:* Milton, Milton and Schurmann)

A Red Guard manifesto

This declaration was issued by students of the secondary school attached to Qinghua (Tsinghua) University in Beijing in June 1966:

> Revolution is rebellion and rebellion is the soul of Mao Tse-tung thought. We are going to strike down not only the reactionaries in our school, but the reactionaries of the whole world too. . . . turn the old world upside down, smash it to pieces, pulverize it, create chaos and make a tremendous mess, the bigger the better! . . .
> Long live the revolutionary rebel spirit of the proletariat!

(*Source:* Milton, Milton and Schurmann)

The Red Guards in action

Red Guards in Canton prepare for a rally.

For many months to come Red Guards went on the rampage throughout China. This is what happened in Changsha, the provincial capital of Hunan during 1966 as remembered by Liang Heng, who was a 12 year-old boy at the time. His student elder sister came home one day:

She said, ". . . . Where do you think I've been all day? I was up on Yuelu Mountain with the Hunan University students trying to get rid of those old monuments and pavilions. And it wasn't an easy job, either. Half the stuff's made of stone. We had to use knives and axes to dig out the inscriptions. Stinking poetry of the Feudal Society! But it's all gone now, or boarded shut."

. . . . Father had found his voice. "How could you destroy the old poetry carved in the temples and pavilions? What kind of behaviour is that?"

"What kind of behaviour? Revolutionary action, that's what . . . ."

(*Source:* Liang Heng and Judith Shapiro, *Son of the Revolution*, Knopf, New York, 1983)

People of the generation of Liang Heng's father were horrified by such Red Guard attacks on China's cultural heritage. They had been brought up with a great pride in and deep respect for their country's history and culture.

Liang Heng's aunt was a scientist who was attacked by Red Guards. She had studied in America where she had met and married Liang's uncle, also a scientist, and she had been a famous botanist at the Shanghai Science Institute. When Liang visited Shanghai this is what his uncle told him:

Then the Cultural Revolution broke. They attacked us both, but she was the major target because she had relatives in Taiwan. They said we worked for the CIA, and proved it by pointing to what they called our "bourgeois lifestyle" . . . she was taken away and locked up . . . . They wouldn't let me see her for months . . . . They had been injecting her with drugs that confused her so much that she didn't know what was true anymore. She told me at the time she couldn't take much more. Then they called me a second time, a week later. It was to get her corpse. . . . Later a worker told me that they had immersed her up to her neck in stinking slime. For three days he heard her screams, and then they stopped. I suppose she ripped her own clothing into strips to make the rope that hanged her.

(*Source:* Liang Heng and Judith Shapiro, *Son of the Revolution*)

As the Cultural Revolution developed, Liang Heng remembered how the Red Guards moved on to their next target:

. . . the arrival of the student Rebels coincided with a change in the focus of the attack, away from intellectuals like my father and toward the Party powerholders. Our old primary school was turned into a makeshift prison for about ten of the top political leaders . . . .

The loudspeaker called us all outside, and in a few minutes I saw it coming. A group of Rebels were in the lead shouting "Down with the

Red Guards parade disgraced officials through the streets. What was the purpose of treating people like this during the Cultural Revolution?

Capitalist Roaders" and "Long Live Chairman Mao Thought". Following them were about ten of the old "leading comrades" tied together on a long rope like beads on a string, their hands bound. They were wearing tall square-topped paper hats inscribed with phrases like *I am a bastard* or *I am a fool*, and around their necks were wooden signs with their names like Fu Dai-zun *Capitalist Roader Power-Usurper* or *Meng Shu-De, Filial Grandson of the Landlord Class* . . . .

(*Source:* Liang Heng and Judith Shapiro, *Son of the Revolution*)

In what ways do you think the Red Guards believed they were helping to achieve the aims of the Cultural Revolution?

What were the main ideas and influences on their actions?

THE CULTURAL REVOLUTION IN INDUSTRY AND AGRICULTURE

Daqing (Ta-ch'ing): the revolutionary model for industry

Daqing was an oil field in the north-eastern province of Heilongjiang (Heilungkiang). In 1964 Mao Zedong had declared it the national model for industry because it was run as he believed all industry in China should be. Its workers were given certain rights, and cadres, or managers and Communist Party officials were not allowed to become a remote and privileged class:

. . . leading cadres . . . will not build office buildings . . . they will live in "makeshift dwellings" or single-storey houses. They will hold no parties and present no gifts; they will neither dance nor put a sofa in their office. They will eat in collective dining rooms. And they will teach their children not to seek special privileges for themselves.

They must persist in participating in physical labour and must never be bureaucrats sitting high above the people.

(*Source:* Hsu Chin-ch'iang: *Hold High the Great Red Banner of the Thought of Mao Tse-tung, Further Deepen the Revolutionization of Enterprises: Basic Experience in Revolutionization of the Tach'ing Oil Field*.)

What conclusions can you draw from this document about the relations between industrial workers on the one hand and managers and Communist Party officials on the other before and during the Cultural Revolution?

Dazhai (Ta-chai): the revolutionary model for agriculture

Dazhai was a poor hill community in Shanxi province in northern China to the southwest of Beijing. Its members had apparently achieved remarkable productivity from their poor and stony soil by their own efforts and without help from the central government. As a result Mao designated Dazhai as a national model for Chinese agriculture in 1964 and everyone on the land was exhorted to "Learn from Dazhai". In 1966 Chen Yonggui, its Party Secretary, wrote an article for the *People's Daily* listing the lessons which Dazhai had to teach Chinese agriculture:

Some people say that to boost the enthusiasm of commune members for work, it is necessary to have recourse to material incentives. I say that we must resolutely uphold the socialist principle of distribution, that we cannot adopt absolute egalitarianism . . . . In other words, we have to recognize some difference, but the differences must not be too great . . . .

(*Source:* Selden op. cit.)

What do you think is the difference in Chen Yonggui's mind between the "socialist principle of distribution" and "absolute egalitarianism"?

What are "material incentives" and why would some people favour them?

THE DOWNFALL OF LIU SHAOQI AND DENG XIAOPING

In August 1966 Liu Shaoqi was demoted from second to eighth in the Politburo: he was no longer the official successor to Mao. The propaganda campaign against him and his views intensified until he was labelled as "China's Khrushchev". In October he wrote the following confession:

I misjudged the situation regarding the proletarian cultural revolution . . . . I took the bourgeois reactionary stand and became a bourgeois dictator . . . . The most fundamental problem was that I did not learn to grasp Chairman Mao's thought . . . . In fact, I often countered Chairman Mao's thought and could not listen to my comrades' correct views. On the contrary, I could easily accept incorrect ideas.

(*Source: Collected Works of Liu Shao-ch'i*, Union Research Institute, 1968, Vol. 3)

Liu was expelled from the Party in November 1968 as "the Number 1 Party person in authority taking the capitalist road". Deng Xiaoping was labelled as the "Number 2 Party person in authority taking the capitalist road", and was similarly brought down. He had been notorious for this saying:

It doesn't matter whether a cat is black or white, as long as it catches a mouse.

(*Source:* Carl Riskin, *China's Political Economy*)

What did Deng mean by his remark about a cat?

THE SHANGHAI COMMUNE AND DIRECT DEMOCRACY

In Shanghai even before the end of 1966 there had been fighting between rival groups of workers. This was followed in 1967 by a "January Revolution" led by Zhang Chunqiao and other supporters of Chairman Mao. They organized workers to throw out the leaders of the city's Communist Party and government and then established a People's Commune with direct democracy and elections on the lines of the Paris Commune of 1870. Mao commented:

If everything were changed into a Commune, then what about the party? .... There must be a Party somehow! There must be a nucleus, no matter what we call it.

I don't believe in elections. There are over two thousand counties in China, and if each county elects two people then there will be more than four thousand people; and if they elect four people then there will be ten thousand – where is there a big enough place to hold a meeting for that many people?

(*Source:* Wilson, *People's Emperor*)

Why was Mao opposed to the direct democracy of the Shanghai Commune?

THE CULTURAL REVOLUTION BRINGS BLOOD-SHED AND CHAOS

Liang Heng recalled the situation one morning in Changsha in the summer of 1967:

... suddenly fifty or sixty men carrying machine guns ran ... toward me. A short man in black carried the flag with the words "Young People's Bodyguard Squad" on it ... I instinctively flattened myself against the wall ... when the men were almost abreast of me they opened fire ....

The enemy was out of sight, but it responded with force. The bullets whizzed through the air ... the flagman fell in front of me and rolled over and over like a lead ball. The flag never touched the ground. Someone caught it and raised it .... Then he crumpled and rolled over and someone else seized it and carried it forward. They never hesitated to take their places in the front line.... The pool of blood widened to within a few feet of my bare toes. I thought I would vomit.

(*Source:* Liang and Shapiro, *Son of the Revolution*)

Why were students willing to die like this?

The most serious episode of disorder broke out in Hubei province between two main groups in the great industrial city of Wuhan, where the river Han meets the Yangtse. Hundreds were killed and industry there was paralysed.

During that summer of 1967 Mao Zedong went on a three-month tour of China and was alarmed by what he found. These are some of his remarks made at the time:

> I think this is civil war, the country is divided into "800 princely states" .... There is no fundamental clash of interests within the working class. Why should they be split into two big irreconcilable organisations? I don't understand it.

(*Source:* Lowell Ditmer, *Liu Shao-ch'i and the Chinese Cultural Revolution*, Berkeley, 1974, and *People's Daily*, 14 September, 1967, quoted in Wilson, *People's Emperor*)

Why was there disorder and why was Mao unable to understand it?

Mao calls in the People's Liberation Army

Mao decided to call a halt. He turned to the one national organization that was still unified and intact to restore order: the People's Liberation Army. The PLA's commander-in-chief Lin Biao had been an enthusiastic supporter of Mao during the Cultural Revolution. He had energetically built up a personality cult of Mao through the army to a pitch that made even Mao uneasy. He had arranged for a "Little Red Book" of Chairman Mao's quotations to be published and it became the bible of the Red Guards. Lin wrote:

> Mao Tse-tung thought must be taken as the yard-stick for everything. In Chairman Mao's thought and instructions, we must have strong faith without any doubt whatsoever at all times and on all questions.

(*Source:* Wilson, *People's Emperor*)

Lin obeyed Mao's directive of September 1967 calling on the PLA to restore order. But it took well into 1968 before success was achieved. Fighting went on for some time between different groups, including serious clashes between armed student factions in Beijing's universities.

In the end Mao sent workers as well as soldiers directly into the universities to end the chaos. The students' days of "making revolution" were over. A much more down-to-earth life was now in store for them.

STUDENTS ARE SENT TO THE COUNTRYSIDE

In the summer and autumn of 1968, 1.75 million school and university students were sent from the cities to the countryside, in effect for good. At first volunteers had been called for and Liang Heng remembered how his sister Liang Fang had gone:

> In January 1968, Liang Fang signed up to go to Jing County in Western Hunan .... She had given up all hope of figuring out the Cultural Revolution, for she had been right one day and wrong the next too many

A Red Guard conductress recites aloud from the Little Red Book to the passengers on a train.

times . . . . But she hadn't lost her interest in social change and the nature of society. She thought that by going to the poorest area she could really investigate China and learn something about Marxism-Leninism and Revolution. She truly believed she could help create a new countryside, a mechanized Communist utopia.

(*Source:* Liang and Shapiro, *Son of the Revolution*)

But initial enthusiasm did not last very long:

Later, after the first groups sent back reports about what it was really like, nobody wanted to go anymore, but by then the program was no longer voluntary, and there was no choice in the matter.

(*Source: Son of the Revolution*)

By 1975 around 12 million young people had been sent to the countryside. It was perhaps one of the most unpopular of all Mao's policies and the great majority became increasingly desperate to return to their city homes. They were followed by Communist Party officials and thousands of intellectuals, including many of China's best-known musicians, actors, singers and dancers.

In what ways did Mao feel the Communist Party had "deteriorated" after 1949?

THE RISE AND FALL OF LIN BIAO

In 1969 Lin Biao was named as the official successor to Mao Zedong. By 1970 however, Lin was apparently the mastermind of a plot to seize power from Mao. His plan, codenamed the "571 Engineering Plan", in which Mao was called 'B52' gave his reasons:

B52 has not much time to go . . . . He does not trust us. We had better act boldly than be captured defenceless . . . . Of course, we do not deny his role in unifying China; it was precisely because of this that during the revolution we gave him the status and support he deserved. Now, however, he abuses the trust and status given him by the Chinese people . . . . He is not a true Marxist-Leninist, but rather one who follows the way of Confucius and Mencius, one who dons Marxist-Leninist clothes but implements the laws of Chin Shih-huang. He is the biggest feudal despot in Chinese history . . . .

(*Source:* Michael Y.M. Kau, *The Lin Piao Affair: Power Politics and Military Coup*, White Plains, New York, 1975, quoted in Wilson, *People's Emperor*)

Do you agree with Lin's arguments and did they justify his trying to overthrow Mao?

Men of the People's Liberation Army bring Mao's thought (and his portrait) to the countryside to enlighten the peasants.

Lin's plot was said to have involved assassinating Mao by planting a bomb in a train on which he was due to travel. But Lin's daughter was said to have betrayed the plot and Lin was officially reported as having died in an aeroplane crash in Mongolia during September 1971 while attempting to flee from China.

DENG XIAOPING AND THE GANG OF FOUR

The power struggle begins

As Mao became older and weaker, a struggle began for the control of China after his death. On one side were Mao's wife Jiang Qing and her three associates, soon to be called the "Gang of Four". On the other were Deng Xiaoping and other veteran Party leaders who were slowly regaining their power in the CCP.

The Gang of Four continually warned against the dangers of the kind of China which they believed their opponents wanted to create. In 1975 one of them, Yao Wenyuan, wrote of the danger that:

> . . . a small number of people will . . . acquire increasing amounts of commodities and money . . . capitalist ideas of amassing fortunes and craving for personal fame and gain, stimulated by "material incentives", will spread unchecked . . . .

(*Source:* Yao Wenyuan, "On the Social Basis of the Lin Piao Anti-Party Clique", *Peking Review*, No. 10, quoted in Carl Riskin, *China's Political Economy*)

Deng Xiaoping took a very different view:

> It is purely nonsense to say that a certain place or work unit is carrying out revolution very well when production is fouled up. The view that once revolution is grasped, production will increase naturally and without spending any effort is believed only by those who indulge in fairy tales.

(*Source:* Chi Hsin, *The Case of the Gang of Four*, Cosmos Books Ltd., Hong Kong, 1977)

By January 1975 Deng had enough political support to be made a vice-chairman of the Party and the first Vice-Premier of the State Council. This made him third after Zhou Enlai (Chou En-lai), China's Premier or Prime Minister, and Mao himself.

THE FOUR MODERNIZ-ATIONS

At the Fourth People's Congress in the same month it was Zhou Enlai who made his famous call for "four modernizations" in two stages: the first to build "an independent and relatively comprehensive industrial and economic system" by 1980; the second, to:

> accomplish the comprehensive modernization of agriculture, industry, national defence, and science and technology before the end of the century so that our national economy will be advancing in the front ranks of the world.

(*Source:* Riskin, *China's Political Economy*)

THE TIANANMEN INCIDENT

The second fall of Deng Xiaoping

In January 1976 Zhou Enlai died of cancer. Of all the CCP's leaders he was probably the most liked and best respected by the people. That was why thousands of them came to Tiananmen (T'ien An Men – Gate of Heavenly Peace) Square in Beijing on 4 April to lay wreaths in his honour. Among them were some placards declaring support for Deng Xiaoping and denouncing Jiang Qing.

During the night all the wreaths and placards were removed. This provoked a massive protest demonstration in the square the following day. The Politburo of the Communist Party then branded the demonstration as a "counter-revolutionary incident" and used it as a pretext to strip Deng Xiaoping of his Party posts. He was again labelled as an "unrepentant capitalist roader" and removed from power.

MAO'S DEATH AND THE FALL OF THE GANG OF OF FOUR

At ten minutes past midnight on 9 September 1976 Mao Zedong died at the age of 83. A little-known member of the Party leadership, Hua Guofeng (Hua Kuo-feng), who had become government premier after Zhou Enlai's death, was Mao's successor as Chairman of the Communist Party's Central Committee.

His first act as China's supreme leader was to move against Jiang Qing and her three colleagues. They were arrested, officially denounced as the "Gang of Four" and later given a show trial after which all received long prison sentences.

HUA GUOFENG'S "LEAP FORWARD"

The Ten Year Plan

The question now was where China should go from here. Hua's speech of February 1978 at the National Party Congress outlined his answer:

In order to make China a modern, powerful socialist country by the end of the century . . . what is of decisive importance is the rapid development of our socialist economy . . . .

There should be a big increase in foreign trade . . . .

"Let 100 flowers blossom, let 100 schools of thought contend" is the basic policy for making China's socialist science and culture flourish . . . .

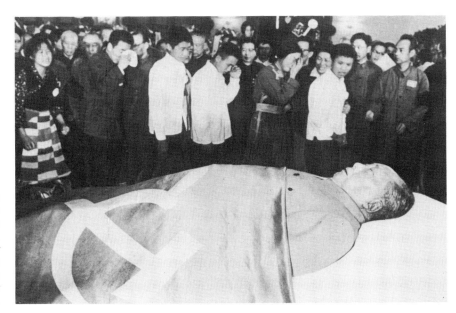

Mao Zedong's body lying in state in Beijing, while his widow Jiang Qing (centre background) looks on. Mao's body was later embalmed and placed in a specially-built mausoleum which was opened to the public.

A demonstration in Tiananmen Square, where the banners proclaim death to the Gang of Four and celebrate the appointment of Chairman Hua.

To accelerate the development of socialist science and culture we must stick to the policy of "making the past serve the present" and "making things foreign serve China". We must conscientiously try to study the advanced science and technology of all countries and turn them to our account . . . .

What would Mao Zedong have agreed with and what would he have rejected in Hua's ten year plan?

What would have been the feelings of China's educated people or intellectuals after reading Hua's speech?

More than 1000 major projects were started in 1978 under the Hua Guofeng plan. These included power stations, railways, chemical plants and a huge new steel plant at Baoshan near Shanghai far bigger than any built in China up to that time. Twenty-two large-scale projects were imported from abroad, the cost of which exceeded China's ability to pay. The total import bill for 1978 reached $7 billion.

READJUSTMENT: CHEN YUN APPLIES THE BRAKES

Chen Yun, the veteran economic specialist in the leadership, had been strongly opposed to the Ten Year Plan. He was in favour of moderate and balanced growth of China's economy, not crash campaigns. He therefore persuaded his colleagues in the leadership to change policy. A new policy of readjustment was announced at the Central Committee's meeting in December 1978. Hua Guofeng's star had clearly passed its peak. The way was now clear for Deng Xiaoping to attempt a second comeback.

ON REFLECTION:

How, in Mao Zedong's view, would the Cultural Revolution contribute to China's development?

Why was it called a "Cultural" Revolution?

Deng Xiaoping's China: The Age of Reform 1978-89

Between 1978 and 1980 Deng Xiaoping won his power struggle with Hua Guofeng. The Four Modernizations remained the recipe for a rich and strong China under his leadership, but he added emphases of his own:

Economic democracy and management

At present the most pressing need is to expand the decision-making powers of mines, factories and other enterprises and of production teams, so as to give full scope to their initiative and creativity . . . . Just imagine the additional wealth that could be created if all the people in China's hundreds of thousands of enterprises and millions of production teams put their minds to work.

Material incentives

As far as the relatively small number of advanced people is concerned, it won't matter too much if we neglect the principle of more pay for more work and fail to stress individual material benefits. But when it comes to the masses, that approach can only be used for a short time – it won't work in the long run.

The need for laws

To ensure people's democracy, we must strengthen our legal system. Democracy has to be institutionalized and written into law, so as to make sure that institutions and laws do not change whenever the leadership changes, or whenever the leaders change their views or shift the focus of their attention.

(*Source:* Speech at the Central Working Conference 13 December 1978, quoted in Deng Xiaoping, *Speeches and Writings*, Second Expanded Edition, Pergamon, 1987)

What are the most important differences between this strategy for development and that favoured by Mao Zedong and Hua Guofeng?

DENG XIAOPING'S MEN: ZHAO ZIYANG AND HU YAOBANG

Since he was approaching 80, Deng wanted to make sure that he would have successors who would continue his policies. He therefore put two of his younger associates into key positions: Zhao Ziyang, who had been Party boss in Sichuan province, became Government Premier replacing Hua Guofeng, and Hu Yaobang became General Secretary of the Party.

DEMOCRACY WALL

On 17 November 1978 a poster was put up on a wall in Xidan Avenue in Beijing criticizing Mao Zedong by name: this was the first time that this had been done in public. The Xidan wall then became famous both inside and outside China as "Democracy Wall" because the Chinese pasted *dazibao*,

Putting up and reading "big character posters" on Democracy Wall in Beijing.

or "big character posters" on it, a customary way of expressing opinions. Such public freedom of expression had not been known in China since the Hundred Flowers episode in 1956.

One poster was written by a young man called Wei Jingsheng and he gave it the title "The Fifth Modernization – Democracy":

Do the people enjoy democracy nowadays? No. Is it that the people do not want to be their own masters? Of course they do. This was the very reason the Communist Party defeated the KMT [Guomindang]. After their victory, did they do what they promised to do? The slogan of People's Democracy was replaced by the Dictatorship of the Proletariat, making a very small percentage of the hundreds of people the leaders. Then even this was cancelled and the despotism of the "Great Helmsman" took over. Then came another promise: because our Great Leader was just so great, the superstitious belief in a great leader could bring the people far more happiness than democracy . . . . But are they happy? Are they prosperous? We cannot hide the fact that they are more restricted, more unhappy, and the society is more backward than ever.

(*Source:* quoted in Roger Garside, *Coming Alive: China After Mao*, André Deutsch, 1981)

Democracy Wall was closed down by the authorities in early 1980. Wei Jingsheng was put on trial accused of revealing state secrets to a foreigner. He was found guilty and sentenced to 15 years' imprisonment.

In June 1981 the Central Committee of the CCP passed a "Resolution on certain questions in the history of our Party since the founding of the People's Republic of China". It was 86 pages long and analysed the history of China since 1949 from the perspective of Deng Xiaoping and his supporters. These are some extracts from it:

The Great Leap Forward

[Failure] was due to the fact that Comrade Mao Zedong and many leading comrades, both at the centre and in the localities, had become smug about their successes, were impatient for quick results and overestimated the role of man's subjective will and efforts . . . .

The Cultural Revolution

The "cultural revolution", which lasted from May 1966 to October 1976, was responsible for the most severe setback and heaviest losses suffered by the Party, the state and the people since the founding the People's Republic. It was initiated and led by Comrade Mao Zedong.

Mao Zedong

Comrade Mao Zedong was a great Marxist and a great proletarian revolutionary, strategist and theorist. It is true that he made gross mistakes during the "cultural revolution", but, if we judge his activities as a whole, his contributions to the Chinese revolution far outweigh his mistakes. His merits are primary and his errors are secondary . . . .

1976: a crucial year

The victory won in overthrowing the counter-revolutionary Jiang Qing clique in October 1976 saved the Party and the revolution from disaster and enabled our country to enter a new historical period of development.

Deng Xiaoping

In 1975 . . . . Comrade Deng Xiaoping took charge of the day-to-day work of the Central Committee . . . . He convened . . . meetings with a view to solving problems in industry, agriculture, transport and science and technology, and began to straighten out the work in many fields so that the situation took an obvious turn for the better.

Why was it necessary to pass and publish this "Resolution"?

How do you explain its verdict on Mao Zedong?

REFORM IN AGRICULTURE

The Household Responsibility System replaces the Commune

During 1978-80 peasants were allowed to have larger private plots and encouraged to increase their output from them. Free markets then grew up in which this increased private produce could be bought and sold. One Party official from Anhui province commented:

What we learned from Dazhai was that Chairman Mao's agricultural policies were a failure . . . . Like most cadres during the cultural revolution, I wasn't impressed by the movement, but we couldn't do anything about it, because it had been the brainchild of Chairman Mao.

(*Source: Financial Times*, 20 May 1985)

This new system was called the "Household Responsibility System" and it later spread throughout China as part of the reform programme. By 1983 it became possible for individual farm households to hire labour, buy and own motor vehicles and farm machinery and to market their own surplus produce. This meant the disappearance of collectivized agriculture as it had been known since the 1950s and the end of the commune as a combined political and economic unit.

Output under the new system increased greatly. The value of agricultural output from 1979-1983 increased by 7 per cent each year. Some enterprising and business-minded peasants became rich from their side-line occupations. In 1985 one of these recalled:

The peasants in my village didn't agree with Chairman Mao's policies . . . I decided to concentrate on manufacturing mats and transporting them by advanced methods . . . .

He employed local villagers to work for him and said he felt no awkwardness about being an employer:

I pay them a good wage. Five yuan a day is more than most of us earned in a month six years ago – and I'm still a peasant, just like everyone else.

(*Source: Financial Times* 20 May 1985)

Chen Yun from his Central Committee vantage-point was concerned about some aspects of the reform:

Some peasants are no longer interested in growing grain. We must address this problem.

Feeding and clothing a billion people constitutes one of China's major political as well as economic challenges, for "grain shortages will lead to social disorder". We cannot afford to underestimate this matter.

(*Source: Beijing Review*, Vol. 28, No. 39, 30 September 1985)

In January 1985, 70 million people, about 8 per cent of China's peasants, were estimated by the Minister of Civil Affairs to be so poor that they were in need of aid.

Why were some peasants uninterested in growing grain?

THE OPEN DOOR POLICY AND ITS EFFECTS

Foreign trade and investment

In 1981 premier Zhao Ziyang called on the Chinese to "abandon once and for all the idea of self-sufficiency".

> By linking our country with the world market, expanding foreign trade, importing advanced technology, [and] utilizing foreign capital . . . we can use our strong points to make up for our weak points . . . .
>
> (*Source:* Report on the work of the government in *China's Economy and Development Principles*, Foreign Languages Press, Beijing, 1982)

What were China's weak points and strong points? How did Zhao expect foreign trade to compensate for the country's weaknesses?

The most drastically new part of Deng Xiaoping's economic reform programme was the policy of encouraging foreign, mainly Western and Japanese, companies to invest money in China in order to set up factories and other enterprises. Special Economic Zones (SEZs) were set up in coastal areas of south-eastern China in Guangdong and Fujian provinces for this purpose. Later, 14 of China's coastal cities were also opened up to foreign investors. The SEZs, according to Zhao Ziyang:

> . . . should boldly introduce advanced technology and methods of management from abroad and make use of foreign capital. Our aim is to promote China's socialist modernization; we should adhere to the characteristics of the socialist system in our work in the Special Zones, and the workers, staff, and other inhabitants should be imbued with socialist morality.
>
> (*Source:* Report on the Work of the Government, 1981 in Zhao Ziyang, *China's Economy and Development Principles*, Beijing, Foreign Languages Press, 1982)

Conditions had to be right for foreign capitalists:

> China stipulates that the income-tax rate for joint ventures and foreign enterprises shall be lower than that in developed countries . . . .
>
> (*Source:* Gu Ming, Deputy Secretary of the State Council, in *Beijing Review*, No. 29, 16 July 1984)

As a result of these policies the number of foreign businessmen and technical experts who came to do business and work in China greatly increased. Eighteen foreign oil companies began exploring for oil in the South China and Yellow Seas and by 1983 1780 foreign companies had invested in China. China also joined a number of international economic organizations such as the International Monetary Fund (IMF), the World Bank, and the Food and Agriculture Organization (FAO). United Nations' aid was used to carry out the national population census of 1982 and World Bank loans were taken to finance agricultural and construction projects.

What is "socialist morality"? Why is Zhao concerned that Chinese working in the SEZs should preserve it?

Deng Xiaoping.

Why did foreign businessmen come to do business in China?

New laws

The idea of law had traditionally been weaker in China than in the West. Under Deng this began to change:

In the past, we did not emphasize developing the legal system, because of our poor understanding of its importance. Through the 10 years of internal turmoil, we have become clear-headed and realized that any lawless act as some did during the "cultural revolution" will bring great suffering to the people. We will not tolerate history repeating itself. The legal system must be improved.

(*Source:* Peng Zhen, in *Beijing Review*, No. 35, 27 August 1984)

China began to pass a whole series of laws. Many governed economic relations with foreigners, for example the "Foreign Economic Contract Law" passed on 21 March 1985. The Chinese knew that foreigners would be unhappy about investing large sums of money in China without the protection of legally enforceable contracts.

Chinese work, study and travel abroad

Chinese workers were sent to more than 50 countries to work on construction and other projects. They were attractive to their hosts because they were cheap while China benefited from the foreign currency which they sent home as well as from the knowledge and experience they gained. Thousands of Chinese students, the majority of them the sons and daughters of Party and Government officials, were sent to universities and technical institutes in Western countries to study advanced science and technology, law, business and management. Hundreds of delegations of Chinese specialists of all kinds made study-visits abroad to find out what the latest developments were in their fields of interest.

Foreigners in China

Besides foreign businessmen and technical experts, millions of foreign tourists took advantage of the open door to see China for themselves. In 1984 almost 13 million of them spent over $US one billion worth of much-coveted foreign currency in China. Hotels were built in all the major cities and scenic places to accommodate them.

Foreign teachers and students also came to China with their news, books and ideas from the outside world. Consumer goods flooded in, especially from Japan. They were advertised on hoardings which previously had only seen political slogans such as "In agriculture learn from Dazhai; in industry learn from Daqing". Especially popular were tape recorders, television sets, video machines and the videos to go with them. Chinese television gave people all over China a window on the world via communications satellites which relayed world news from countries like America and Britain.

Bourgeois liberalization and spiritual pollution

By 1983 the party leadership had become seriously worried about the effects of the Open Door policy both on Party members and on society generally. On 31 October Zhu Muzhi, the Minister of Culture, explained:

There are two kinds of spiritual pollution, one, in theory, that violates Marxist principles, and propagates the value of human beings, humanism, and socialist alienation . . . [the other] is within literary and art works, and in performances propagandizing sexual, depraved, terrifying, violent things and the kind of stinking bourgeois life-style that consists of looking for fun, drinking, sleeping, and being happy.

(*Source:* Judith Shapiro and Liang Heng, *Cold Winds, Warm Winds*, Wesleyan University Press, 1986)

There followed a campaign against "spiritual pollution" conducted by those in the Party who were opposed to many aspects of Deng Xiaoping's reform programme, above all the Open Door Policy. It lasted for three months and was eventually wound down because it shook people's general confidence in the reform programme: they were afraid another Cultural Revolution was on the way.

The *People's Daily* of 21 December tried to calm these fears:

What is worth paying attention to now is that some have expanded the elimination of spiritual pollution into daily life, have said that wearing high heels, curling hair, wearing new-style clothing, growing flowers, and so on – all things beautifying life – are also spiritual pollution. This is wrong. People should not mix up spiritual pollution with changes in material and cultural life, and even more, they should not interfere excessively with different customs of life . . . .

(*Source:* quoted in *Cold Winds, Warm Winds*)

Many senior Party and Government officials and their children were more interested in the opportunities to make money under the Open Door. They took full advantage of their privileged positions to do so. This particularly worried Chen Yun:

Party and administrative cadres and their children swarm forward to do business. According to surveys in a dozen provinces and cities since the last quarter of 1984, some 20,000 various companies have sprung up, a considerable number of which collaborate with law-breakers and unscrupulous foreign businessmen . . . .

The decadent capitalist ideology which is characterized by the "worship of money", is exerting a serious corrosive influence on our party's work habits and social mores.

(*Source: Beijing Review*, 14 October 1985)

Argument and debates about the Open Door policy continued. In October 1984 Deng Xiaoping said:

If we practise isolationism and close our doors again, it will be absolutely impossible for us to approach the level of the developed countries in 50 years.

(*Source: Beijing Review*, Nos 7-8, 18 February 1985)

The economist Li Honglin saw the problem as follows:

When our door is opened, some dirty things are bound to come in. What shall we do? There might be two methods. One is to close the door again ... [but] ... the dirty things outside might still come in through the cracks.

The other method can be called "filtration". It is just like installing air filters on the doors and windows to remove gas and dust ... some dirty things are bound to slip through.

Even the cleanest person's face will have some dirt because he does not live in a vacuum. There is nothing to be afraid of when the face gets dirty. The only thing to do is to wash it more often.

(*Source: Beijing Review*, Vol 28, No. 13, 1 April 1985)

What foreign influences were China's leaders most opposed to and why?

Do you agree with Li Honglin that it is possible for China to "filter out" such influences while maintaining an Open Door policy?

Reform of industry

Having reformed agriculture and China's economic relations with the outside world, the next main target for reform was China's industry, much of which was located in towns and cities.

On 20 October 1984 the "Decision of the Central Committee on Reform of the Economic Structure" stated:

... the enterprise should be truly made a relatively independent economic entity and should become a producer and operator of socialist commodity production that is independent and responsible for its own profit and loss ....

(*Source:* BBC Summary of World Broadcasts, 22 October 1984)

Such reforms:

... badly need ... managers, who are both knowledgeable in modern economics and technology and imbued with a creative, innovative spirit .... We have large numbers of veteran comrades ... who ... have made great contribution to our socialist construction .... But they are getting on in years .... Our present urgent task is to promote boldly thousands of young and middle-aged managerial personnel and take steps to train them ....

(*Source:* BBC Summary of World Broadcasts)

Price reform

Reform of the price system was a key element in the reform programme. Tian Jiyun, a vice-premier of the State Council explained why:

... China's current price system is quite confused. The prices of many goods neither reflect their value nor the relationship between supply and demand. More often than not, goods that should have high prices are not expensive and those that should have low prices are not cheap ....

(*Source: Beijing Review*, No. 4, 28 January 1985)

The effects of the reform were not long in coming:

Dramatic price rises in Beijing have prompted grumbling from many residents .... Pork rose from 2.20 yuan per kg to 2.98 yuan, beef from 2 yuan to 4.40 and eggs from 2.20 yuan to 2.60 yuan.

(*Source: Beijing Review*, No. 20, 20 May 1985)

Prices continued to rise. A young woman official in Hunan province observed:

I do not care what anybody says, prices have risen much faster than income this year and last year ... I feel it every time I want to buy something for my baby or when I want to buy a wider variety of vegetables.

(*Source: Financial Times* 18 December 1986)

Why was China's price system "confused" and what were the problems caused by this?

What risks were China's leaders running in trying to change it?

Population

By 1980 it became clear that even with an average of two children per family, China would have more than 1.5 billion people by the year 2050 but no extra land to feed them from. This was a recipe for perpetual poverty. China's leaders therefore saw how urgent it was not just to control the population but to reduce it.

Their answer was a "one-child policy" designed to make China's population peak at 1.2 billion by the year 2000 and fall to 700 million over the twenty-first century. Severe penalties were introduced for couples who had more than one child. This was much easier to enforce in the towns than in the countryside, where the policy had unintended and tragic consequences. This is from a report of an investigation carried out by the Women's Federation of Anhui province in 1983:

... in some rural areas there is now a serious disproportion between male and female babies, and the ratio of female to male babies has dropped even to a low of 1.5 in some areas .... The main reason is the malpractice of drowning and abandoning baby girls under the influence of the remnant feudal ideology that regards men as being superior to women. In 1980 and 1981, in a certain production team in Huaiyuan county, more than 40 baby girls were drowned.

(*Source: People's Daily* 7 April 1983, quoted in BBC Summary of World Broadcasts)

What could the long-term consequences of one-male-child families be in China?

STUDENT UNREST AND THE DEMOTION OF HU YAOBANG

In November 1986 student protests and demonstrations began in Shanghai and spread to universities in other big cities including Beijing. There in December students of the Teachers' University took to the streets shouting "We want liberty". In Hefei, Shanghai, Nanjing and Hangzhou others shouted: "We want freedom, We want democracy . . . ."

In January Hu Yaobang made "self-criticism of his mistakes on major issues of political principles and collective leadership". Among his mistakes, according to a Hong Kong source, were opposition to criticism of spiritual pollution and bourgeois liberalization, leniency towards the students and recommending "high consumerism" in economic matters.

His request to resign as General Secretary of the Party was unanimously accepted by the Central Committee and Zhao Ziyang, the Premier, was made acting General Secretary in his place.

Why do you think that the students were demonstrating at this particular time?

What conclusions do you draw from the dismissal of Hu Yaobang?

POLITICAL REFORM GOES ON THE AGENDA

In August 1987 Deng Xiaoping said that the Central Committee had been considering speeding up the reform and the opening to the outside world and in particular political reform:

Generally speaking, reform of the political structure involves democratization, but what that means is not very clear.

It was Zhao Ziyang who specified what political reform meant and how it was to be carried out later in the year:

Political restructuring involves primarily the reform of the leadership system. Without resolving the confusion between Party and government functions and the usurpation of government role by the Party, it is impossible to unfold the reform of the political structure as a whole . . . .

(*Source: People's Daily* 26 November 1987, reprinted in *Beijing Review*, December 1987)

What should be the proper roles of Party and government in China according to Zhao and how should they fit together?

ZHAO'S BLUE-PRINT FOR CHINA'S FUTURE: OCTOBER 1987

On 25 October 1987 Zhao Ziyang delivered his report to the 13th National Congress of the Communist Party. It included the following:

Ever since the Third Plenary Session of the 11th Central Committee, we have been carrying out a strategic plan for economic development. This plan involves three steps. The first step is to double the GNP of 1980 and solve the problem of food and clothing for our people. This task has been largely fulfilled. The second step is to double it again by the end of the century, thus enabling our people to lead a fairly comfortable life.
The third step is by the middle of the next century to reach the per capita GNP level of moderately developed countries. This will mean that modernization has been basically accomplished and that our people have begun to enjoy a relatively affluent life.

(*Source: Beijing Review* 1987)

JUNE 1989: THE TIANANMEN MASSACRE

In May 1989 President Gorbachev of the Soviet Union made an official visit to China. He had become a hero to China's students and intellectuals because under the slogans of *perestroika* (restructuring) and *glasnost* (openness) he was introducing in his country some of the political freedoms which they were demanding in China. When he arrived, Beijing's students occupied Tiananmen Square in their thousands demanding freedom, democracy and a crackdown on corruption. This was a deep humiliation for Deng Xiaoping and his colleagues before China and the whole world.

The demonstrations continued in Beijing and other Chinese cities for days after President Gorbachev had left. Hardliners in the CCP came to believe that chaos would result unless they acted. The People's Liberation Army was therefore ordered to end the demonstrations by force, and on the early morning of Sunday 4 June Chinese army tanks drove over and crushed the sleeping bodies of students in Tiananmen Square. Troops opened fire on the unarmed crowds. Hundreds were killed including some soldiers, torn to pieces or burned alive by enraged citizens who fought back.

The crackdown succeeded. Deng Xiaoping congratulated the troops for crushing what he called "the counter-revolutionary rebellion" and said that the trouble had been started by "a very small number of people" whose aim was "to overthrow the Communist Party and the socialist system . . . [and] transform the People's Republic of China to a bourgeois republic". Many of those who had taken part in the demonstrations were arrested, tried and executed. A few managed to flee abroad.

The Tiananmen massacre marks a totally different stage in the relations between the Chinese Communist Party and the Chinese people and particularly China's intellectuals. Never in the history of the People's Republic since 1949 had the CCP ordered the army to turn its guns on the unarmed population. What effects this action will have on China's political system and its long struggle to achieve power and wealth is impossible to foresee. Many observers believe that little significant change will take place until Deng Xiaoping and the other old men of the current leadership are dead.

Glossary

APC	(Advanced Producers' Co-operative, also called "Semi-socialist" or "Lower Stage" APCS): groups of about 20 peasant families or households who pooled their land, labour, working animals and tools. They were introduced in the first stage of collectivization of agriculture during 1954-5 and replaced in 1956-7 by the larger Higher Stage Co-operatives, which contained around 160 families
big character poster	(in Chinese *dazibao*) put up by private citizens in a public place to air opinions and express criticisms, often about Party or government officials or Party policies. They have been the main means of expression of uncensored public opinion
bourgeoisie	the middle or capitalist class, which as Marxist Communists see it owns a country's means of production as private property and uses them to exploit the labour of workers. It does not share out fairly the wealth which the workers mainly create and it controls the government in its own interests
cadre	(pronounced ka-der) generally means a full-time official of the Communist Party or of the central or provincial government
Capitalist Roaders	the label used by Mao Zedong and his supporters in the Cultural Revolution (1966-1976) to describe Party leaders like Liu Shaoqi and Deng Xiaoping who were in favour of Soviet Russian policies and practices and of such things as profits and bonuses in industry and private plots for peasants. Mao believed that they were turning the Communist Party into a privileged élite remote from ordinary Chinese
Communism	a society in which, according to the Marxist view, the means of production are owned by the whole people, there are no social classes, and there is no exploitation of man by man. The economy works on the principle of "from each according to his ability, to each according to his needs". Mao Zedong, echoing the Chinese Classics and Kang Youwei, the radical scholar-official of the late 19th century, sometimes referred to it as the "Great Harmony"
Confucianism	the system of social and political thought derived from the teachings of Confucius. It was the official ideology of Chinese state and society from the Han dynasty (206 BC—AD 221) until 1912 and still influences people's thinking and behaviour in China and countries which have been influenced by China, such as Japan
feudal	the term used by Chinese Communists to describe Imperial China, when the country was governed by scholar-officials or bureaucrats
Gang of Four	Mao Zedong's closest supporters during the Cultural Revolution, comprising his wife Jiang Qing (the only woman), Zhang Chunqiao, Yao Wenyuan, and Wang Hongwen. They were given a show trial in 1980 for their alleged crimes during the Cultural Revolution and all found guilty
Guomindang (Kuomintang/KMT)	the Chinese Nationalist Party founded by Dr Sun Yat-sen after the fall of the Qing dynasty in 1912. It was China's main political party until the Chinese Communist Party seized power in 1949. Its leaders and many of their supporters then fled to the Chinese island of Taiwan (Formosa)
Hundred Flowers	from a classical poem "Let a hundred flowers bloom, let a hundred schools of thought contend". The words were applied to the short period during 1957 when Mao Zedong allowed and encouraged freedom of expression
Imperialism	in China means the political and/or economic domination of the weaker countries of the world by capitalist countries such as the United States and Western Europe
Intellectual	in China, refers to people with at least a secondary school education. They there-work with their brains and have generally looked down on people who work with their hands. University-educated people in particular have traditionally seen them-

selves as China's real elite. As such Mao Zedong always regarded them as a threat to the CCP's monopoly of power. That is why they were one of the main targets of the Cultural Revolution

"left" deviation
a policy or action which is intended to bring about an extreme degree of equality or "absolute egalitarianism", often regardless of practical possibilities

Marxism
the political ideology originated by Karl Marx. It predicted the revolutionary overthrow of the capitalist system by its industrial workers who would then establish a socialist and later a communist society

Marxism-Leninism
Marxism as developed by the Russian revolutionary V.I. Lenin, who led the Bolshevik Revolution of 1917 and founded the Soviet Union. He argued that it was not necessary for a backward country like Russia to go through a capitalist stage before establishing socialism

Marxism-Leninism-Mao Zedong Thought
the official ideology of state and society in the People's Republic of China. Defined by the CCP as "a correct theory, a body of correct principles and a summary of the experiences that have been confirmed in the practice of the Chinese revolution, a crystallization of the collective wisdom of the Chinese Communist Party"

Mutual Aid Team
groups of three to five peasant households, later of up to 20, which pooled their labour, working animals and tools. Peasants were encouraged to join these after the Land Reform of 1950 to improve the efficiency of Chinese agriculture

Nationalists
members of the Guomindang or Nationalist Party

People's Communes
introduced during the winter of 1957-8, they were the largest unit into which peasants were organized after 1949. They began to be dismantled after Mao's death in 1976 and by the late 1980s had almost disappeared

Production Brigade
the middle organizational unit of a People's Commune between the production team below and the commune itself above. It was often a natural village and a former Higher Stage Co-operative of around 160 peasant households

Proletariat
the industrial working class, which Marxism predicts will overthrow capitalism. They own no property like the bourgeoisie, but have only their labour and skills with which to earn their living. The literal meaning of the term for proletariat in Chinese is "propertyless class"

Readjustment
the term for the economic policies which were introduced by Liu Shaoqi and Deng Xiaoping after the failure of the Great Leap Forward of 1958 and again by Deng after the death of Mao Zedong in 1976

Revisionism
the policies followed in the Soviet Union after 1956 by Nikita Khrushchev and his successors. Mao Zedong believed that they were bringing about a restoration of capitalism in the Soviet Union

Socialism
in Marxist thought the lower stage of Communism. In it, as in the higher stage of Communism, the means of production are owned by society as a whole. But labour remains the measure of distribution of the goods and services which people need under the principle: "from each according to his ability, to each according to his work"

Yuan
monetary unit. China's currency, called Renminbi (RMB) or People's Currency (as the UK's currency is called "Sterling"), is divided into 1 yuan, 10 jiao and 100 fen

Timeline

DATES	SIGNIFICANT EVENTS IN CHINA	SIGNIFICANT WORLD EVENTS
1949	1 October, Mao Zedong proclaims the People's Republic of China (PRC)	**1944-5** United Nations established Cold War begins
1950	China signs Pact of Friendship and Alliance with the Soviet Union; becomes member of the Communist Bloc	**1947** India and Pakistan become independent
1951	Three-Anti and Five-Anti movements against political and economic corruption begin	**1948** Transistor invented NATO established
1952	Land reform completed State Planning Commiss on established Nationalization of private business	US explodes hydrogen bomb
1953	First Five Year Plan announced	
1954	Agricultural co-operativization (APCs) begins	
1955	First Five Year Plan officially adopted	**1955** Warsaw Pact set up
1955-6	Mao speeds up agricultural collectivization	
1956-7	"Hundred Flowers" period of freedom of expression	
1957	"Hundred Flowers" ended; Anti-Rightist Movement begins	**1957** First earth satellite launched (Soviet Union)
1958	Second Five Year Plan announced Great Leap Forward begins People's Communes introduced	European Economic Community founded
1960	Sino-Soviet dispute begins, Soviet experts withdrawn from China Mao Zedong in "retirement". China ruled by Liu Shaoqi and Deng Xiaoping	**Late 1950s-1960** Asian and African former colonies gain independence
1960-62	"Three Bitter Years" of natural disasters and famine. Between 16 million and 43 million estimated deaths China explodes first atomic bomb	**1961** First man in space (Soviet Union) **1961** Japan introduces "Bullet Train"
1964 **1966**	Third Five Year Plan officially begins. Mao starts Great Proletarian Cultural Revolution. Student Red Guards on rampage	**1965** Vietnam War begins in earnest
1967	Mao calls on Marshall Lin Biao and People's Liberation Army to restore order	
1969	China explodes first hydrogen bomb. Students sent to countryside permanently	**1969** First man on moon (USA)
1969 **1970**	Lin Biao named as Mao's successor China launches first earth satellite: it broadcasts the song "The East is Red"	
1971	People's Republic of China (PRC) takes China's seat in the United Nations replacing the Republic of China (Taiwan)	
1972	Lin Biao plot against Mao discovered. Lin reported dead in plane crash fleeing China US president Nixon visits China	**1972** President Nixon signs SALT 1 (Strategic Arms Limitation Treaty) with Soviet Union
1973	Deng Xiaoping re-elected to CCP Politburo; struggles for power with "Gang of Four"	**1973** USA withdraws from Vietnam

ATES	SIGNIFICANT EVENTS IN CHINA	SIGNIFICANT WORLD EVENTS
75	Zhou Enlai calls for policy of "Four Modernizations"	
76	Tiananmen incident. Second fall of Deng Xiaoping Mao Zedong dies; succeeded by Hua Guofeng Gang of Four arrested (on trial 1980-1)	
78	Hua Guofeng's Ten Year Plan announced; blocked by Chen Yun. Decline of Hua begins Deng Xiaoping becomes most powerful single man in China. Brings in supporters Zhao Ziyang and Hu Yaobang	
979	PLA no match for Vietnamese army in China's brief invasion of northern Vietnam "Household Responsibility System" introduced in agriculture USA recognizes the People's Republic as legal government of China	1979 Mrs Thatcher becomes Prime Minister of Britain; begins programme of reforms based on belief in economic individualism and free markets Soviet Union sends army into Afghanistan
980	"One-child family" population policy announced	
981	Zhao Ziyang calls for "Open Door" policy to West	
983	"Campaign against Spiritual Pollution" Western influence	
984	Britain agrees to return Hong Kong to China in 1997 Special Economic Zones set up to attract foreign industrialists China begins to pass laws to encourage foreigners to do business with China Reform of China's industry announced Thousands of Chinese start to go abroad to travel, study, and work. Thousands of foreign tourists and businessmen come to China	
985	Inflation becomes a problem	1985 Mikhail Gorbachev becomes leader of Soviet Union. Acknowledges that the country cannot catch up with the West under existing political and economic systems. Starts programme of reforms under slogans of *perestroika* (restructuring) and *glasnost* (openness)
986	Student demonstrations for democracy	
987	Fall of Hu Yaobang Deng Xiaoping and Zhao Ziyang propose reforms of China's political system	
988	Pace of reform slows because of unrest caused by rapid price rises	
989	President Gorbachev visits China. Student demonstrations end in massacre in Tiananmen Square in June	Mr Gorbachev announces Soviet Union will withdraw from Afghanistan Unrest among non-Russian states of Soviet Union as a result of Gorbachev reforms

Sources and Book List

Primary Sources As China has been a totalitarian state since 1949, most primary sources relevant to this book are in Chinese, almost all of them being official publications issued by the Chinese Communist Party or by other official bodies, containing only what the CCP or government want people to know. Because of the lack of independent media, historians and journalists need to seek out the truth. They can also get independent opinions from foreigners (like diplomats) living in China, or from Chinese citizens themselves, although giving information to foreigners is usually treated as a crime by the authorities.

Listed below are some of the books available which contain translations of primary sources, together with some first-hand accounts of China since 1949, as well as general histories and economic surveys.

Ed. Franz Schurmann and Orville Schell, *China Readings*, Vol. 3, "Communist China", (Penguin Books, 1968)

Ed. David Milton, Nancy Milton and Franz Schurmann, *China Readings*, Vol. 4, "People's China", (Penguin Books, 1977)

Ed. Stuart R. Schram, *The Political Thought of Mao Tse-tung*, (New York, 1963)

Ed. Stuart Schram, *Mao Tse-tung Unrehearsed, Talks and Letters 1956-1971*, (Penguin Books, 1974)

Foreign Languages Press, Peking 1965 & 1977, *Selected Works of Mao Tse-tung* Vols. I-V

Biographies Stuart R. Schram, *Mao Tse-tung*, (Penguin Books, 1967)

Dick Wilson, *Mao The People's Emperor*, (Futura Publications, 1980)

General Histories John K. Fairbank, *The Great Chinese Revolution: 1800-1985* (Chatto and Windus, 1987)

Immanuel C.Y. Hsu, *The Rise of Modern China*, (Oxford University Press, 2nd edition, 1975)

Edwin O. Reischauer, John K. Fairbank and Albert M. Craig, *China: Tradition and Transformation* (Allen and Unwin, 1979)

Witold Rodzinski, *The Walled Kingdom*, (Fontana Paperbacks, 1984)

Economic Surveys Christopher Howe, *China's Economy, A Basic Guide*, (Granada, 1980)

Carl Riskin, *China's Political Economy: The Quest for Development Since 1949* (Oxford University Press, 1987)

Xue Muqiao, *China's Socialist Economy*, (Foreign Languages Press, Beijing, 1981)

Contemporary Witnesses

John Fraser, *The Chinese, Portrait of a People*, (Collins, 1980)

Roger Garside, *Coming Alive: China After Mao*, (Andre Deutsch, 1981)

Liang Heng and Judith Shapiro, *Son of the Revolution*, (Knopf, 1983)

William Hinton, *Fanshen: A Documentary of Revolution in a Chinese Village*, (Penguin Books, 1972)

Edgar Snow, *Red Star Over China*, (Penguin Books, 1972)

Edgar Snow, *Red China Today*, (Penguin Books, 1970)

Index

In the Index entries are given in Pinyin, with the Wade-Giles form in brackets. Entries are also printed in Wade-Giles, which refer the reader to the main, Pinyin, entry e.g. Teng Hsiao-p'ing, see Deng Xiaoping.